Four
of Love

- A Novella

VIVEK SHARMA

Cover design by Sunill Kaushik of Ink Studioz

In memory of my dad

To love or have loved, that is enough. Ask nothing further.
There is no other pearl to be found in the dark folds of life

-Victor Hugo
.

CONTENTS

A Note to the Reader

One balmy evening last spring me and my wife sitting in the cozy living room of our fifteenth floor condo were getting profoundly rapturous at the prospect of attending the twenty-fifth grand reunion of our school batch and our romantic nostalgia stemmed from a very innocent fact- We were the only "alumni-couple" in the whole batch.

Suddenly breaking our reverie, my recently teenaged daughter walked inside the room and switched on the television set. For an upcoming school project she wanted to watch *Discovery Channel* which was about to air a documentary on the life of US soldiers in a war.

It was a well-made documentary covering almost all aspects of a soldier's life, but after watching it a part of me felt something was amiss. I was particularly intrigued by a quote in that documentary which came from the commanding general of the coalition troops in the *First Gulf War*. He said "It doesn't take a hero to order men into battle. It takes a hero to be one of those men who goes into battle".

I couldn't have agreed more with the General but something in that statement made me sad. It made me sad because I felt there was so much more to the concept of heroism which never gets reported or quoted. I can say so, as my first cousin whom I am very close to, retired as a Commander from the Navy, and we've had long discussions on the "valor and heroism" of a soldier, and these discussions have led me to believe that truth is not always what it seems to be, just like (even when it comes to a war), heroism is not *only* about a soldier going out to fight. It's much more than that.

Heroism is the power to ride all storms, whether in life or in war. But the anatomy of heroism with respect to a war is somewhat intriguing. No doubt fighting for your country needs loads of valor, but for a soldier, heroism is not as much about going into a battle as it is about facing life after the battle. And that needs a lot of courage because love needs a lot of courage and in my humble opinion the DNA of heroism is nothing but love. Those who have it, live. Those who don't, perish. Notwithstanding their valor in the war zone.

It so happened the very next morning a professor from my wife's college, from where she did her MD, came visiting us and though it was not my first meeting with the professor but since the documentary of the previous night and the quote from the General were fresh in my mind, for the first time I could actually see, what the lady must have gone through in her life.

Across a span of ten years she lost both, her father (a Lieutenant Colonel) and her brother (a Major) with the army, in armed conflicts.

But she had coped well in life considering the nature of her loss. Truly heroic!

And that made me think- Here I was, fortunate enough to have a life where a girl who meets me in high-school and with whom I get romantically involved, gives me much more than what my teenage sought satiety of hormonal surge desired. I end up getting a life where twenty six years after that first meeting, I have the bliss of sitting in my living room making plans with her to go back to the same place where it all started- our alma-mater, to attend our silver jubilee grand reunion.

But my story could have been different. Hadn't my dad refused to sign the parental consent form, there were pretty decent chances that I might have joined the armed-forces like many of my batch-mates, like that army Major or like that Colonel or like those soldiers shown in the documentary.

Isn't it a matter of few crucial moments gone this way or that way which decide the fate of many things in our life. But whichever way life may take us, the show has to go on and in the end where we reach is always a function of the choices we made along the way.

As they say, pain is inevitable but suffering is optional. Which means there must be something in some of us or (being an optimist) maybe most of us, which gives us the power, the life-fuel, to survive all storms. .

I wanted to explore it through a story which is what I have done here. The story is fictional but the underlying emotions are universal as the story itself is inspired by some true man-made events.

This story is about six people from three generations whose lives got entangled in the eye of a storm. A storm which stood to take from them everything they cherished. This is a story about their hopes, despairs, joys and sorrows and the ultimate destiny which awaited them beyond the storm.

Provided they could ride and sail through it.

The story unfolds through *four* letters written across a span of 22 years.

The first one is from a US marine who writes to his beloved from the war zone in *Operation Desert Storm*, longing to be with her because of a letter he has just received. A story which commences from a night of passion at *Assateague* beach- *Virginia*, and moves on to a war front at one of the most forlorn places on earth where a "soldier-lover" tries to understand what the game is about.

The second one is to a mother from a daughter- a soldier's fiancée, who understands many things about her relationship with her mom when she discovers something about herself. A story where her newly-born future lifts her to latitude where she finds the courage to redeem with her past.

The third one is from a father, an ex-marine to his son who is about to graduate from *Yale Law School*. A letter which is as much about the past as it is about the future, where a father gets the chance to give to his graduating son the best gift any father could ever give.

And the fourth and final one where a son's life is touched by the profundity of love- changing his life forever. A letter which brings redemption to a group of people who lost everything in a war which took place because of the greed and arrogance of a few people who thought that war is the instrument through which justice prevails. But in the end the only thing which prevails is love, which is the common thread connecting these four letters.

I hope you enjoy reading them.

Vivek Sharma

Not Exactly Excerpts

The missile ripped through the tail of his F/A-18C fighter jet and it coughed profusely with smoke billowing out of its lungs. Walter knew it was time to abandon the aircraft which lost altitude at an alarming rate. He ejected, bailing out in the enemy territory moments before the plane went into flames. The parachute opened with a jerk, taking him down into *Iraq* occupied *Kuwaiti* airspace. Walter knew it was a *heat-seeker*; an IR guided SAM, which meant he urgently needed to direct his flight members to make a break turn and initiate a decoy flare to beat the surface to air missile seeking them. While in parachute descent he used his survival radio and sent several distress signals. There was nothing more he could do and as he sunk into the belly of darkness pressing on him from all sides his whole life flashed out in front of him.

"Is this the end?" he thought.

Just before taking off from the base a few hours back he had written to Julie, promising her to be back soon, to take care of her and their yet to born child.

And never before in his life had he broken a promise, ever! Not even once.

"No, this can't be it, not now...No", he thought, before saying to himself, "Come what may, I would make it. GODDAMNIT, life cannot betray me... Not now".

The deep dark hole of the wintry night swallowed him as he thought about Julie's eyes.

Just before his feet touched the ground there was a sharp twinge in his ribs and he knew it was a bullet. He could feel the warmth of his blood as it oozed out from him and he saw himself falling.

His body became light, so light that he floated and though the night was as dark as the Stygian depths of an ocean, but yet he could see Julie standing in front of him with her arms wide open, and with a smile in her eyes.

Darkness enveloped him as his eyes closed.

"Take him in", said the Iraqi Major to his soldiers.

**

Julie was stupefied by her feelings since morning.

She could feel something inside her change the moment they told her she was pregnant.

The boulders she had nurtured in her head from childhood just melted away filling each and every pore of her body with warmth she had never felt before, and she wondered "does motherhood changes everything?"

She wrote to Walter telling him that their trip to Assateague beach just before he left for his war was really "*productive*".

But writing to Walter couldn't soothe her nerves the way she thought it would and once again she felt it building up inside her, that intense longing, breaking through her self-imposed barriers of the past, swaying her completely in its intensity this time.

And then it exploded through her eyes, the suppressed yearnings of past *twenty* years and she felt a debilitating pain tear through her heart.

"Where are you", she could hear herself utter these words for someone with whom she seldom spoke. The veil of her pretense was no more and all she wished for in that moment was to hug Grace and feel her. There was so much to share and she was already late.

She wondered about the sea-change in her feelings in less than twenty four hours as she sat down to write to Grace, her first letter in past fifteen years.

Perhaps motherhood changes everything...

**

He knew the response was simply fantastic, maybe one of the best ever anywhere in the world for an Art Gallery inauguration. An array of glitterati from the British high-society graced the opening, jostling for space with the crypto Illuminati of the art world. James was very happy as it appeared *Amour* was the right theme and Edinburgh the right venue for his fifth gallery in Europe.

A smile played on his lips as he replied to the Washington post journalist, "I have always felt that one can never go wrong with *Amour or* Love, be it life or be it a theme for an art gallery."

As he came out he thought about Peter who was graduating from Yale in a few weeks and he wondered if the time had come to share with his son what he'd waited for all these years.

What could be a better gift for his son on his graduation day?

He smiled at himself as he said to the cab driver "*Prestonfield* please".

**

He had read the letters, both of them, more than three times in past one hour, and was about to read them again when he heard the yell, a loud one, of the kind which comes from a large group gone berserk. He looked out of the bedroom window of his four-teenth floor suite at the *Hall of Graduate Studies*. They were assembling in the garden below to celebrate as it was that time of the year at *Yale* when some two hundred and fifty five *Yalies* after surviving the "*Dead Week*" and the anticipatory stress of the final results, were finally going to embrace glory by getting their graduate degrees at the commencement ceremony which was to happen at the *Lanman* Center.

Peter was about to step out to join his buddies in the garden below, when the letter arrived. It was from his dad.

And going through the contents of the courier changed his entire world. He never knew some couriers could do that- change worlds.

Being in a space of gratitude towards life's prowess to give always gave him more, at times much more than he wished for or even deserved.

But this was incredible. Here he was, counting his lucky stars for being fortunate enough to get what he had always wanted- a law degree from a place like Yale and the priceless experiences of past three years on the campus giving him everything a man could ever ask for.

But the letter from his dad changed all that.

There is no limit to life's capability to surprise you. The letters proved it conclusively.

"Where are you dad, I need to talk to you", he thought as he dialed his father's number.

**

.

1st

From Walter to Julie

**And now these three remain: faith, hope and love.
But the greatest of these is love.**

Corinthians 13:13

Letter from Lieutenant Walter to Julie

30th Jan 1991, Theater, Iraq

Dear Julie,

This indeed is a day of reckoning. A day when a self-professed agnostic like me wants to believe in something which he never did before.

Providence.

Which embraces me every-time I reach the fag end in my journey? And no wonder nine out of ten times it works through you? Like it did today again through your letter which I read once, and then once more, and then one more time and then I had just one urge-to somehow cover these 6000 miles and be with you, even if it could be just to hug you once.

To listen to your heart which now beats for both of you, to look into your eyes and see your inner world where our love child is breathing. To just hold you and make you understand what this moment means to me. Oh *jazzits*, I wish I could be with you right now!

I have fallen in love with *United States Postal Service* for connecting us with our loved ones, getting us letters in this war zone. Today when I got yours some ten minutes back, I just went bonkers, so much so that the guy who brought it to me said, "Lieutenant, you grin like a jackass eating cactus. What's it about? Your sweetie got a bun in the oven?"

I told him "Oh Yes" and just kissed him. Wish you could see the expression on his face.

You know something; suddenly I have this really strong urge to get hitched. The moment I am back, the first thing we'll do would be to walk down the aisle, with *Diana Ross* & *Lionel Richie* playing *Endless Love* in the background or maybe something classical, like *Pachelbel's Canon in D*, or if you wish maybe a live bravura rendition by some local virtuoso band. But let's do it and at the same place, *Assateague beach*, where we conceived our child. Now how would that be? Wouldn't it be awesome to have a beach wedding walking barefoot on the sand, before saying "I DO" to each other?

Guess what? I had a premonition that night itself. It was a strange night in many ways. *Operation Desert Shield* had failed and all of us at the base, at *Oceana,* knew it was just a matter of time when the order would come beckoning us to the scene of action and that's why we had decided to simply elope for a few hours to steal some moments for ourselves, to kindle our passions, before saying goodbyes.

You remember it? I know you do.

That unstated anxiety and the disquieting expression on your face. That deceitful mask of gaiety you adorned. I know it stemmed from the realization that the battlefield could be an abyss of infinite possibilities- all unpredictable.

And when I said "Jule, Come-on, it's a small insurgency, not like World War Three", you just said one thing. "I know Walt, but I love you, and you are all I have got".

And then you melted me with those looks, making me hungry, inflaming my passions to a state where I had just one desire- to take whole of you in my arms to love you, comfort you and tell you that I'll be fine. Do you also feel that in those few moments we lived and experienced reality the way it has always connected us, giving us a glimpse of the truth about us?

But wait a minute. I suddenly realize I used these two words- 'truth' and 'reality', which of late have started bothering me a lot? I feel they come out of the dictionary just to play hide and seek with me.

When I am with you these words stay with me and I feel I know them and understand them. At least I presume so. But it's very different here. Here, these two words leave me to go and hide somewhere and I am no longer sure of what they are actually up to. Here these words sound at best divergent and at worst superfluous.

Truth is *Saddam's* forces captured *Kuwait* and truth is that the mighty system of which I am a small part, decided that war is the only solution to the oppression which *Saddam's* regime perpetrated on *Kuwait*. But Reality is I have no clue how this war is actually going to change all that on the ground.

How? I mean actually how?

Truth is President and the Secretary try their best to indoctrinate us on the rightness of this battle, but reality out here is people in *Baghdad* kill each other for flimsy reasons and petty amounts and "We", the saviors of freedom, add to the count of bodies carbonized and incinerated by bombs and bullets.

From what I have seen here, *truth* flies from the muzzle of our bullets and bombs, and *reality* from all that they touch. That is how it works here. And this isn't a war in the conventional sense, as we have a very high tech "death machine" deployed here against Saddam which drop bombs and takes his men apart.

But I hope whatever this is- war for justice or peace or for God knows what, when we achieve our object-ive, something far more important prevails, something which the people living out here haven't seen from a very long time and something which all of us living back home take for granted.

Peace!

I expect this war would bring that. Because peace alone would determine the kind of world our baby would get to breathe in. And I yearn it to be enduring so that there is no need ever for a Secretary or a General or a President to ask an American again, to throw bombs at other human being in the name of freedom and duty.

That's why despite all of this my heart actually wants to believe President *Bush* when he says *"If anyone tells you America's best days are behind her, they're looking the wrong way."*

Oh-Heavens! Here I go again. I think I am getting seriously affected by what they call the impermanence of life circumstances? Something which my flight from *Virginia* to the Theater of operations at *Iraq* brought upon me, an abject contradiction in my cir-cumstances- from the warmth of your embrace to the inferno of this war.

Let's talk about something more spirited. Something like that evening when I was back from *Oceana*, convincing my commanding officer Zubin to give me *twenty-four* hours, just *twenty-four* hours of away-time from the base, to be with you. You remember how desperately you waited for me and the moment I reached home we just bolted off to *Chincoteague* Island.

What a place it was! I can still feel the misty freshness of the *Assateague* beach air tingling on my skin. You remember how windy it was that evening. We had put up our tent at the far end of the beach towards the end of the whole walking loop. The winds created a beautiful symphony with the waves and there was not a soul in sight, just miles of beach with sea breeze creating strange noises of all kinds.

It was a full moon night and the moon was out to fondle everything. In the sky, it courted the night, trading its glow for the night's darkness.

In the ocean, its light caressed the undulating waves which roared with the intensity of a virgin seeker destined to explore, knowing fully well it has to surrender in the end, to its nemesis, the shore.

And in your eyes, it smiled at me, with your radiance mingled in its glow and in doing so it did something else too. It made you so vulnerable and me so ecstatic in the same moment.

Your lips quivered to say something in vain as no words could convey what the soul beseeched. I lifted you in my arms and felt that quiver kissing me and trying to communicate with me. That exquisite innocence of your looks; I could literally feel it swarming every single pore of my body and in your eyes that night I saw the reflection of my whole life.

It wasn't about your beauty or even about my passions to consume and get consumed by you. I feel it was about the spaces, the voids in me which you filled by a simple touch of yours or by your glance or by your smile... and the best part is somewhere deep inside I had this feeling that even you felt the same.

Guess our souls got entwined.

The warmth of your love, the halo of your body wrapped around me under a sheet in our cosy tent on that beach. Nothing else mattered. Your soul met mine on your lips on your body, in every nook and corner of yours in all those spaces which were there to be filled in by the other. Our bodies met to fill those spaces in our soul. You held me forever.

You resisted, not to save yourself but to burn with me without any precondition, eternally. I wanted to have you, but you still resisted to further ignite the raging fire to such an intensity which could subsume everything; so that nothing remained in that moment to be consigned further. To make it absolute and that's why the culmination was blissfully insane.

We've had so many memorable trips to *Assateague* over past one year but looking back I feel what happened that night was something really mystic. We became 'One" like never before as if there was a whole universe inside of you trying to reach out to me and today I understand why the consummation of our passion was so beautiful and so mind blowing that the uninhibited cry of joy which came at the culmination made even that pair of sea gulls squawk giving us a screeching cry.

The sea roared against the black horizon. Life on that beach slept in the lap of the dark night which played with the twinkling stars. You slept in my arms as I smoothed your hair thanking God for making this world with you in it for me. I kissed you thanking you for bringing order to this chaos called me; for making me complete.

I kept looking at you for a very long time till the fire outside went out and don't remember when I felt asleep holding you in my arms.

Destiny choosing to bequeath us with posterity giving us the biggest gift a man and a woman can yearn for, the gift of creating life through love. Now I understand why that night was so esoteric. Maybe nature has a way on deciding the timing for such life events and I am so happy our child picked up those moments to arrive in our lives.

Today after reading your letter, that evening came flashing past my mind, but being where I am right now, in an unknown land taking lives of unknown people in the name of duty sometimes makes me wonder whether I am doing the right thing. I hope I am. So that if one day my child asks me why I did what I did, I could take pride in sharing my experiences with her.

But frankly speaking at the moment I don't know exactly what the truth is. I cannot say with absolute conviction what this war is really about!

They tell us this war is about freedom. It was quite inspiring when just before starting from *Virginia* I heard the Secretary's speech "…..Kuwait's needs to be free of *Saddam* and of all the oppression he has perpetrated. The elite forces of United States lead a coalition to thwart and preempt his nefarious intentions, his evil designs to annex *Saudi Arabia*. I have no doubt that we will defeat him sooner rather than later……"

No doubt Iraq needs to be contained but there is more to the story. I had some inkling like many others but got a real primer on it the night when our squadron was preparing for deployment and I bumped into James while entering the mess for dinner. The air inside the mess was all charged up by the excitement driving many of us over the edge. After all, for most of us it was the very first time at a real war.

I asked James "Did you hear the Secretary? Any idea how bad is it out there?"

James smiled while he answered "Looks like we should be able to wrap up pretty soon. After all can't allow him to hit the American way of life".

"Which means?" I asked him.

James got excited as he spoke, "Come on Walts. I bet you know that if *Saddam* succeeds he would be sitting on 40% of oil reserves of this world, so this war is as much about Kuwaiti or Saudi citizen's freedom as it is about *Oil*. To ensure that the American way of life is preserved."

Our short conversation ended there and it was only when l landed here and saw things firsthand with my own eyes I realized, that those who plunged thousands of soldiers like me into this war never learned any lessons from *Vietnam*. Lessons about not entering in somebody's backyard messing around in their civil war expecting to come clean without inflicting collateral damage on people who have no role to play in that war.

To people like me this war is not about oil or freedom or redemption or any high fancy stuff. To tell you the truth, at a very basic level it boils down to only two things for a soldier- Killing and saving oneself from getting killed which many a times means more killings.

Period!

But I try hard to make myself believe what I am fighting for would usher in what they say it would- justice and peace or whatever. It's really important for me personally as I am the one, one among many, fighting for this so called noble cause by bombing people out here. And who are these people? Most of the times they are Saddam's forces who need to be contained for obvious reasons, but many a times we also hit starved & confused souls, who are completely clueless about what they stand for.

It might look odd putting it like this but being a pilot often saves me from coming face to face with the inferno of destruction which I unleash from air sitting in my F/A-18C. I learned it the other day when I met Josh, a private, who was brought to the field medical unit for first aid as he was injured in an operation when some *Jihadist* ambushed his squad and opened fire. He got away with minor injuries but was under severe trauma.

One of his squad members told me "We were crossing a market in our Humvee when suddenly our front tyre got stuck in something. Josh and one more private got down to have a look and suddenly there was an explosion followed by a barrage of bullets. It came from behind a small hillock adjacent to an open ground. Our *M2HB* roared for next couple of minutes firing more than 1000 rounds.

We got them. Four *Iraqi* commandos, taking all of them down."

"Must have been a narrow escape", I said.

"It was indeed. But seven civilians also came in the line of fire and succumbed to the bullets. They were bad... I mean completely torn by the 0.50 caliber bullets of the heavy machine gun", the private said matter-of-factly before he was summoned by someone.

I went to Josh who lay on the bed all bandaged up. There was something about him, maybe his gaze, which made him look like an Egyptian mummy staring since eternity into oblivion.

"How you doing man?" I asked him.

There was no reaction from his side as he stared ahead without blinking his eyes even once. Then suddenly he turned his gaze towards me and blurted out "Eyes... his eyes. They came out... with half of his face torn ..."

I tried to comfort him by putting a hand around his shoulders but he went on, "that old guy came running towards the Humvee...with his left forearm gone...I saw him ... I saw his eyes before he went down... His eyes were asking me WHY? Why me?"

The nurse asked me to leave Josh alone and I came out of the tent but not before realizing firsthand that many of these guys out here, the civilians, are trapped in this inferno with no clue how to come out of it. They obviously have a big "Why?" written over their face when a bullet or a splinter of a bomb takes them (or a part of them) apart.

I know as a soldier of US armed forces it is a privilege and honor to be at the theater of Operations but what's also true is this being very different from our sorties which we do when we are not in a war zone. Here we are not firing at dummies. They are real people, flesh and blood humans, so it's very important at least for me personally to be sure of the rightness of my actions.

After that meeting with Josh some strange things have started to happen. Often, when I close my eyes to sleep, I see faces. Horrified, burnt and pleading faces. Asking me not to put an end to the dreams they have nurtured for their kids, for their families, for themselves.

And I wake up feeling sorry for everything.

The other day I met James and told him about what I was going through as I felt he is far better at dealing with situations like these. He told me "You are not alone in this. Many of us have our own demons to deal with. But I feel all of us should clear our conscience whichever way we can. I do it by telling myself that somebody has to do the job, to establish the spirit of freedom for the majority."

I want to believe him as it's important for me to feel what I am doing is the right thing to do. Fingers Crossed!

See, yet again I bother you with these talks, which I shouldn't especially when our love is blossoming in you.

So our baby arrives in October. I don't know much but one thing I know is that a *Libran* child is cute with chubby cheeks and a smile which can fill an entire room. I hope our child takes your smile. As far as heart goes no doubts there as with so much of love in her genes I think she might sing back a love ballad when we sing her a lullaby.

Oh My! I have already assumed our child is going to be a girl. I have this very strong feeling that it would be a girl. What do you say? I know you always wanted a girl and so did I.

I hope this war comes to an end soon. I hope the co-alition wins this war or better sense prevails and *Saddam* and his *Republican Guards* move out of *Kuwait* so that I can come home and take you in my arms. It's been just a couple of weeks since I landed here but so much has happened in this short time, it feels as though I was always here.

Have you thought about names? What about *Sarah* if she's a girl? I would love it if we name our princess *Sarah*. Sarah means pure and happy and that's all I really care about. Who can understand and appreciate the importance of harmony and peace better than a soldier on war-front. Sarah appeals to me as that one name which could foster all this. What do you say? If we have a boy, I'll go by whatever name you decide for him. I think that is fair enough, isn't it?

And by the way, why don't you ask your Mom to come and stay with you for next couple of weeks, at least till the time I am here. I think our mission out here should be accomplished in next one month, although that does not bring-in the kind of elated feeling I thought it would. I am not sure if the adrenalin junkie in me who always wanted to join the forces is still alive. If not completely, some part of it is certainly dead. You fight one war and come to know war can never be adventurous. I am no *Buddha* here, but right from day one of the air strikes, many of my friends and colleagues are coming back in body bags and some of them are even missing. There is a whole array of military jargon which floats around: KIA-Killed in Action, MIA- Missing in action, BNF- Body not found and many more.

Sometimes I wonder how a complete, living person can go missing. I mean they do every day here and I myself have witnessed many of my colleagues getting reduced to those three alphabets here- MIA. But how can one whole, throbbing, yearning life go missing. I mean NO! It's insane and cruel and I feel it's never a person, a soldier who alone goes missing. What about his or her spouse, partner, mom, dad, son or daughter. All of them become MIA with him or rather MIL-*Missing in life*, FOREVER, and God forbid sometimes without any closure. Their lives change forever. I know it. Life is never the same for them again.

The war statistics are all wrong. For every missing soldier they should count each and every loved one of the soldier in that MIA list.

Can't help talking about all this. Guess being in the middle of a war changes so many things. It changes you from the inside, especially when you are not a witness or a victim but a perpetrator of that war.

Tell you what; at times the feeling is absolutely killing. It kills a part of you.

Now please don't start worrying about me. You know how much I love my job and being part of the most elite force in this world. It's only the carnage, the sufferings I have seen here recently which make me sad and sometimes confused. Of late I have also begun to understand the dichotomy that a soldier is a harbinger of peace. I know it sounds weird- soldier and peace! But the logic is that soldiers make Armies and Armies have capabilities which sometimes act as deterrent to a war.

If there was one wish I was to make for our child, just one, guess what that would be. That she learns early in her life the whole show is about love and nothing else, and come what may- the game has to be played from the heart, for that is the only way to play it well, never leaving hope- whatever be the situation or circumstances. I hope as her parent I could help her reach there.

You must be wondering how philosophical your Walter has become of late. Believe me, being "me" at the moment, being a soldier in the middle of all this makes you philosophize. After all what is philosophy? The dictionary which I have access to says it is *the rational investigation of the truths and principles of being, knowledge, or conduct.* So it's not all that difficult as theater gives you ample stuff to go on that trip. Yes, it does and it's not only me but many of my buddies out here who are in the same zone. Sometimes it's hard to believe the silences which exist in the midst of all this nerve wrecking action. Even when all of us here are together, we are actually alone at a certain level, thinking about so many things which we are witnessing for the very first time.

OK, enough about the war. Let's talk about Sarah. So Love is one endowment which I think she would have in her genes, what else? I guess being the daughter of a soldier she might have in her a fighting spirit, resilience, the will to survive and the capability to look at life directly in the face and say " BEHOLD, here I come."

Wow! Wouldn't that be fantastic? I hope that she has in her the empathy to listen to her heart and the courage to follow what her heart says. What else one needs in this life?

And honey after I come back I might give a serious thought to what I want to do next. No, I am not quitting the Forces, not yet, but I need seriously think about all that I have already seen here and am going to see in next couple of weeks. So many things have happened and I guess it's about time I analyzed all of it before deciding on the future course of action.

But one thing is for sure, I want to be around you. I want to take real good care of you, ensuring that the journey of bringing our child in this world is something which we cherish throughout our lives and when she comes I want to give her all that I can give, feeding her, changing her nappies, giving her a bath, seeing her grow from a toddler to a young girl who would go out with me on bike trips, out in the sun surfing on a beach.

I don't want to miss out on anything- absolutely anything. We would go on vacations together. Of course we'll need to plan it based on her school calendar and my job and your office, but I want to travel, serious and well planned travel -all three of us. One day she will grow up and like a bird will fly out in the sun, first college and then finally a nest of her own. But till that happens I want to give her all those moments which neither I nor you had, when we were growing up.

When she grows up into a young girl and we grow old, I hope she would look back at her growing up years with a blissful feeling in her heart. I hope she cherishes most if not all the moments, spent with her parents. Nothing would be more precious to her than the love which seeps into her heart, her soul through us. I hope she finds a man who loves her for the person she becomes and gives her much more. So that when it's pack-up time and we have to take a walk, we do it rest assured that our Sarah would do well when we are gone.

Yes, I know I am getting a bit mushy here but I know the value of this feeling, that we played our part well as a parent. I learned it looking into many eyes which got closed here because of this war and honey; let me tell you, I still feel their anguish of not being able to do all that they wanted to, for those who stayed behind in this world.

Promise me you will really look after yourself well till I am there to take charge. Call your Mom. I know Grace and you have a difficult relationship but I also know both of you love each other a lot and even you know that, don't you? She would feel good if you call her asking her to come and stay with you. After all it's her first grandchild and there is nothing else which can bring her more happiness than taking care of her pregnant daughter. And don't you think this is the best chance to foster those bonds with your mom which because of so many reasons neither of you could ever nurture?

Tonight our squadron is scheduled for a major field operation and James is also a part of it. We were talking this evening when your letter arrived and he grew a bit nostalgic remembering all those wild parties we used to have back home. He asked me to give a big "Hi" to you and teased me had he met you before me; today this letter from you would have been addressed to him and not to me.

I know the poor chap could never get over the crush he had at you at school and dreams of you even now.

So I told him "Buddy, better reach out to her before me in next life."

But don't tell the poor soul, his heart would be crushed. I'll beat him the next time too, if there is any such thing.

Love

Walter

2nd

From Julie to Grace

My children are blessed and will be mighty in the land.

Psalm112:2

Letter from Julie to her Mother Grace

15th Jan, 1991. Jacksonville, FL

Dear Mom,

I got it.

"Life is moments. Lots of them. Each one having the power to fill the spaces inside our being, provided we allow them to give us what they want to. What they can."

Remember these words?

I got it today and I got it why I never understood the essence of these words which you said more than five years ago. How could I? One needs to be prepared to understand certain words. And I for sure wasn't that day.

But today is different. Today the clearing got splashed with light, heralding the essence of your words to my whole world- the one which lives inside me and the one I live in. An essence so very beautiful and so true indeed!

It happened when they told me my test results are positive and I am going to become a mom, and in that splash second I felt something else too. Something, which I never felt before in my life.

How do I define it?

It was a very strange feeling- pristine yet scary. Feeling of a baby breathing inside my womb, taking shape, waiting to come out in this world, and you might find it hard to believe but the very first thing which came to my mind was you, your deep blue eyes saying so many things to me, your tender touch caressing me silently.

And I started missing you terribly!

As you had rightly said, sometimes it takes just a moment for those inner voids to get filled. In one sweeping moment my inner world transformed into something so beautiful, *the world of a newly born mother*, completely swaying past the bitterness of an old rebellious daughter. For me it was indeed a moment of re-birth.

And then I prayed.

For a healthy baby and for the courage required in the days to come to face the real miracle-*the commitment to be a good parent, a*nd when I did that, suddenly I had a very strong urge. To reach out to you and touch you and tell you that "I love you Mom". Something which I always wanted to do but for the contretemps of my past which ensnared me- preventing me from listening to my heart.

And then I realized how angry I have been all these years. Simmering from inside like the magma underneath a volcano waiting to erupt.

The fact that what we think about ourselves becomes the truth for us, actually happened with me, alienating me from myself and estranging me from you- who loved me the most. The feeling that lingered on all the time was - *"My mother does not loves me"*. But today when Walter's love is taking shape inside my womb, I don't know why suddenly everything seems so clear.

It's been just a few minutes since the doctor told me I am pregnant and his words had such a sonorous effect- lifting me to a latitude from where looking at the future I can understand my past.

But your daughter could understand this only when she was re-born as a soon-to-be mother. Perhaps entering into the state of creating life endows you with the perspective to understand your connect with those whose flesh and blood got you into this world. What I feel for my baby today, you must have felt the same- or maybe more, for me.

It all started like a fairytale, those lovely early childhood days, when I was everything for you, your entire world. You called me *"Julie my princess"* and without fail this princess mornings started with a hug in the bed from her mom and then very gently you would take me out of the bed. I remember so many mornings when you would sing and dance with me and overjoyed by my ecstatic wails of laughter you would swing me in the air and I would giggle from ear to ear always knowing I would safely land in your arms. It was our daily play- singing, dancing and you cooking for me all of my favorite recipes.

Unfortunately those days didn't last long. Dad for me was always an enigma during those growing up years. I would see him once a month or maybe two, and that too stopped after some time. He became just a concept for me, a character in a story, a prince in my imagination fed by you, kept alive by you, existing more in my mind then in the real world.

But there was no way we could ascend on a descending escalator. With each passing month those precious moments I so much looked forward to have with you and dad, started to reduce, till one the day when they totally stopped.

They had to. The way I understood it then, the prince in the story left for a fairer fairy and suddenly you had to face that harsh reality which you always tried to hide from me and life thereafter changed for both of us.

You, who had never stepped into an office or worked before had to suddenly worry about everything - food on the table, bills, rent for the house... The way I saw it, you were so angry with dad you refused to take even a single penny from him. And I was equally confused and angry with you as I felt you were as much responsible as him in our family getting disintegrated. I longed to be that princess who you said I was, but not all fairy tales have a happy ending. Dad literally walking out on us crushed my heart completely and I outgrew my belief in fairy tales pretty early in life.

He took with him the ground beneath my feet as life was not the same after he left. From a homemaker you had to metamorphose overnight into a bread earner and the only way to do that was by shunning the confines of our home and stepping out into the cruel world.

A world which sucked you completely in, leaving no time to spend with your princess. You worked crazy hours- a full time job in the logistics department of *Winn-Dixie* supplemented with a part time job of taking art classes in a neighborhood college. I so desperately missed my early childhood days and over a period of time withdrew into my shell blaming you and dad for everything.

The world I lived in was never enough- ever! Because I always wanted more thinking life wasn't fair to me in anything taking more from me than it gave. There was a time when my irritation with the world was absolute making me completely morbid and as a consequence completely blind to whatever you did for me- which always fall short of my expectations from you. I could never see your pain, the vast emptiness and blackness of your horizon. It was me, me and me all throughout these years.

It's so strange today when I have a life taking shape inside me I am able to understand how wrong I was in blaming you for everything. How could I not understand there was no other way you could be under those circumstances? You did all you were capable of doing and much more to put our lives back on track and doing that you missed all that a girl aspires for in her life.

You tried really hard to reach out to me, to kiss my soul but my soul was blind and blind souls can't be kissed. But today when your grandchild kissed that blindness away from my soul exalting me to the status of a creator- a mother; I could feel something blossom inside me, something which was always dead and something which could have made all these years so different.

I wish I could see it then, the way I see it now.

When they told me today that I am pregnant, my first and foremost emotion about my baby was to protect her. I closed my eyes and imagined that she has already arrived and I am holding her close, close enough. She looked so small and vulnerable and suddenly this world looked so big and self-obsessed I felt I would always have to be around her to ensure she gets the best of everything in her life.

But then I thought, even you must have felt the same for me when I was born, when I was growing up. I have everything in my life today one aspires for- a caring partner who dotes on me all the time, who not only loves me but understands me as a person, and values my work giving me that creative space which I need as a professional musician. I have a home full of all comforts, sheer abundance of all things required to make life beautiful.

But you had none of it Mom. Neither emotional nor any kind of financial security. Dad robbed the former by walking out on you for another woman and your self-respect came in the way of asking him for the latter. But yet you gave me everything, every material comfort, a good education, skills to be independent and so much more which I never appreciated all these years. I always saw what was not there. I always felt unlike other moms you were never around me when I came back from school. That I had to eat alone as you always worked long hours. I could never understand that you had no life of your own because the only thing you ever did was to work, because you wanted to give me everything.

I never realized love isn't only about being around to cuddle, many a times it's about being there to provide, to take care of things- come what may.

How could I not feel your pain of being away from your child, leaving her in crèches, arranging for her to be dropped and picked up from school? But today when I am nurturing my child in my womb I can clearly understand that helplessness and pain you must have felt because of not being able to spend time with me.

And then that horrible incident of my childhood happened and my whole world collapsed gnawing out even the last shreds of love and affection which I had in some deep recess of my heart. It was hideous; the most horrific thing which can ever happen to any child, but being my mom you must have felt deader than any dead in this world. And the worst part is that forget about completing with it, till date we could never discuss it even once, as despite you trying your best I closed all doors of communication with you.

He was such a charmer, *Bobby*, our new next door neighbor whom we met for the first time in our apartment elevator. He was indeed an urbane-sophisticate by virtue of his suave mannerisms and debonair style and that's why when he invited us for tea that evening at his place, despite not being very keen, you could not say No to him.

I had read somewhere that "what we long for and cannot attain is always dearer than what we have already attained." Right since my early childhood days my soul yearned for fatherly love which I never got and such was my depravity that I had absolutely no clue of the feeling, the bond which a girl shares with her dad. But the longing to have a father figure in my life was very much there.

Bobby was the first male who touched my life after dad who practically speaking was more of a notion, an apparition for me than a real flesh and blood person. And here was this charming *Cathay Pacific* Pilot and his stewardess wife replete with so much bonhomie. To a person like me for whom life was all about shedding tears in anguished solitude of a broken family, even a small display of family hood was *manna* for the soul. Bobby & his wife Alicia looked so perfect to me with their impeccable sense of humor and caring looks and gestures. I liked being at their house and grew extremely fond of their company after meeting them only once.

You already know how in due course of time we became good family friends visiting each other's homes and sometimes when you would get late from work and if Bobby was at home, he would help me with my homework. He would play with me, telling me interesting anecdotes from the aviation industry, feeding me with amazing cookies home baked by his cute wife.

But what you might not know is how it all started. When Alicia went to Texas for a couple of weeks to be with her mom, some strange things started to occur. A bit of touching here, slight fondling there, which I could not understand initially and got totally confused as Bobby did it quite nonchalantly while helping me with my homework, without batting even an eyelid. He made it look so casual and normal as if it was the most normal thing to do to a kid. I felt totally trapped and did not have the nerve to tell it to anybody including you.

It went on for more than a year and I was so small and innocent I never realized it was the violation of the grossest kind of my body. He was such a smooth talker, a charmer and storyteller and I was so fond of him initially that my fondness combined with my na-ivety came in the way of realizing what was actually happening. But when I understood what it actually was, it was too late. I felt horrible, cheated, violated, dirty and extremely angry, raging with anger and frus-tration and most of it was against you, because I felt all of it happened right under your nose and you could not save me. It was very painful for me to think how I changed from a lively, playful child to a reclus-ive quiet and sullen teenager.

And one fine day when God knows from where I got the courage when he tried to go for it again taking me for granted, all hell broke loose and years of oppres-sion and mental torture burst all barriers opening the floodgates. Mount St. Helens erupted inside me and I spewed vitriolic molten lava on him hitting him with whatever I could lay my hands upon, shouting and crying all the while. Neighbors came and so did Police as someone had called 911 seeing the blood ooze out of his nose and head.

The Sergeant informed you and you came home rush-ing from office. l still remember the cry you gave out seeing me in that condition, followed by the never ending silence with air totally blown out of your lungs taking away the last bit of strength from your body. In your already dark and gloomy life this was perhaps the biggest jolt, the biggest trauma, something which was beyond you- the fighter woman, to come to terms and deal with.

You held me close to your heart, kissing me on my face, caressing me on my head and I clung to you tightly but the shock was too much for you to bear. Perhaps you were a bigger victim than me in all that happened.

Suddenly you collapsed. I was out of my wits seeing you in that state and shook you hard but you would not move. They immediately took you to the hospital and I had the good sense to call Richard who did not answer so I left a message on his answering machine.

It was a cardiac arrest and when I saw you in the hospital with tubes coming out of your body I realized beneath that outward shield of anger which I always wore when you were around, deep inside I loved you a lot. It was just that I could never express it in front of you. We had such a difficult relationship mom, and today I realize that most of it was created by me and a bit of it by our circumstances.

But there is always light at the end of the tunnel as everything comes to a pass after running its due course. You and Richard were seeing other at the time and the way he looked at you and took care of you and handled me showed that he really cared. He was nothing less than an angel sent for two oppressed souls. But life was tough, a bitch for us and you wanted to be doubly sure before saying yes to him.

There is something called destiny and so a month after coming back from the hospital you and Richard got married and for the first time I felt the inklings of living in a real family. Richard took Bobby to task and kept no stone unturned to ensure that he was charged with felony and sentenced for seven years.

There was some sense of justice being done but the trauma was too deep, and a part of me could never let it go when I thought about the whole incident. So much had happened in past few years of my life. I had insecurities of all kinds and you were the only one till Richard came into our lives whom I could hate...or love.

I devoted myself completely to academics and other activities which became my savior. The wound started to heal but the scars were still there and at times I had bouts of anger especially when I was alone as to why things happened with me? Why was I the only child in our whole neighborhood, in our whole goddamned list of acquaintances who got raped? And most of all why could you not protect me?

I could never forgive you.

A part of me still had doubts about your love for me? But the other part? When I lay quiet at night I would wait for you, but when you would come and kiss me I would pretend to be asleep. You would tuck me in properly and sit by my bedside for some time before saying *"good night honey, mommy loves you a lot"*, and then you would switch off the night lamp and silently walk out of my bedroom closing the door gently.

In those moments I wanted to rush to your arms to tell you *"Mom, I love you too"* but I could never bring myself up to do that and next day again my veil of anger would come up, my shield against you and the whole world. The dark night made me dark too but the worst part was even the morning sun could never take away that darkness from my being.

But I was lucky to have very good friends in my life right from my middle school, especially Walter with whom I could share anything even then. I guess that's what saved me from going into acute depression after that horrible incident. You took me to the best therapists in Jacksonville and they did help me in getting the strings of my life back in my hands but I know my biggest support system were my friends Walter and James. I so desperately wished to feel the support, the love which I had in my life because of my mom which I could never do explicitly, although I knew in my heart you loved me the most. I could never see your pain, your limitation and most of all life's total unfairness towards you in almost everything.

But today, my baby has given me the perspective to understand what you must have gone through all these years and how you must have felt when your only child couldn't feel your love for her. I was such a difficult child and you were such a wonderful mom. You never let my shield of arrogance against you come in the way of taking right decisions for me and my career. Right from my early days when I was about four years of age you had discovered my flair for instruments, especially piano and you got me enrolled in a piano class which was the only place in the whole word where I could be myself and all throughout those years till Richard came into our lives, you never let me miss a class not a single one. No matter what I would say to you, yell at you throwing tantrums, you would never give it back to me and take all my curses, tantrums so patiently and just tell me *"OK Baby, shall we go now?"*

Nobody, I guess not even a father can do this; reciprocating the evil and Machiavellian forebodings of a hormone-surged child with kindness and benevolence. One needs a mother's heart to understand these seemingly spiteful but attention seeking shenanigans of a child.

How could I doubt you mom all these years? How could I doubt your love? I understood it today when life has exalted me to the position of a mother. Today I understand love is absolute, you cannot love more or less, you either love somebody or not.

And you loved me.

But when you loved me so much, what happened on the way? Why didn't I feel loved enough all these years? Why I always felt like a victim?

The answer lies in my womb today. All these years I judged you only by your shortcomings never appreciating the goodness, the love and care you had in your heart for me. One has to understand love to allow it to come your way. Only when I felt that enormous amount of love growing within me did I understand how complete love is.

All these years I conveniently overlooked how much of a dedicated parent you were. Today I understand what you have done for me. You sacrificed so much for me by not committing to Richard, one of the most fantastic humans beings in this world till the time you were confident that he would fit in, in our family, as my father.

Now, that my angel is coming in this world I can feel the responsibility that comes along. Walter is in the war zone. I just hope that he is back by my side to help me take care of this biggest miracle which life has bestowed upon me, the miracle of parenting.

I wonder that my child who will come through me will obviously have all my love and care yet she will blossom on her own having her own thoughts. Would I be able to give her all that I should, resisting the urge to give her my thoughts, my mind, so that she is not a better version of me but the best version of herself?

The way you did it for me, giving me the freedom to be myself. You did that for me, actually quite wonderfully but because of my difficult circumstances I could never value what I got from you.

I know purpose of life is to flow, to go forward without dwelling in the past but somewhere deep inside me I strongly feel that my tomorrows lie buried in my yesterdays and until I complete with them, I would never be able to do all that I need to for my child.

But mom, that would not happen the way it should, unless I tell you that I have always loved you all these years, always, and if I could do even half of what you did for your child, I would consider myself blessed . And I have a feeling my child will never feel my love till I feel my mom's, the way it actually was.

I woke up around Six AM today, and as I looked out of my bedroom window I saw the sunrise taking place which reminded me of the times of my childhood when looking out from my bedroom window at magnificence of the rising sun, I could make contact with the love which lay dormant in my subconscious for you. But it would happen only in those sunrise moments and then the hullabaloos of daily life would fade that contact.

I hope that my child does good, learning to perpetuate this contact, whenever it happens and make it last forever, acknowledging what her heart or inner voice says to her. In the end it's all about listening with honesty and with courage so as to pursue happiness, the ultimate goal of life.

Please come and stay with me mom. I promise you this time I won't pretend I am sleeping when you'll

come to my room to say good night and cuddle me in
the sheets...

Your daughter

Julie

3rd

From James to Peter

I can do all things through him who strengthens me.

Philippians 4:13

.

Letter from James to his Son Peter

10th May, 2013, Edinburgh, UK

Hi Pete,

So this is it boy. A couple more days and you would be on that podium for a rendezvous with your destiny.

Can't wait to say "Hail Yalie", in fact both me & Nancy are eagerly waiting to see you on that dais on your graduation day, from where your chosen journey into this world would begin.

It would be the culmination of your childhood dream and a truly momentous occasion for me and your mom, when our Pete graduates *summa cum laude* from Yale.

Over the past fifteen years two things in my life never changed - traveling and writing to you, and while living my dream of an art nomad I must have written more than a hundred letters to you from across the globe. But today as I write this one from Edinburgh, where I and your mom are inaugurating our 15th Art Gallery, which is the fifth one in Europe, there is something which makes timing of this letter absolutely perfect. Maybe as perfect as the smell of the fallow after the first spell of rains.

And I say so, because the theme of our *Edinburgh* gallery is *Amour*- love, and what better time than today to share with you world's best love story which I know of. Something which I wanted to do much earlier, but as they say *"Everything is preordained"*, including timing of sharing stories.

Now this isn't "any" story, like the ones I often tell you in my letters or share with you on the dinner table at home- which I suddenly remember we haven't done from quite some time .

No, it's not that kind of a story. Rather this is an extraordinary story about two very special people from my life. So special that I can say they got me baptized into the only religion they believed in, changing my life forever. It was indeed baptism by fire in more ways than one for many people involved and today on the eve of *Amour's* inauguration, I thought I should share it with you.

It is the story of Walter and Julie.

Walter was the most enchanting person I came across in my life. He was my buddy from *Jacksonville,* where we grew up together in the same neighborhood, went to the same school, had a big fight the very first day to sit next to Julie- the new girl in our class and by the end of a week ended up asking her out, of course separately, but on the very same day

And as was to happen, both of us tasted our debut rejection too, the very same day.

Julie, our nemesis, was an enigma in every sense of the word. There was something about her which caught one's imagination. She had long auburn hair flowing across her heart shaped face with lustrous curvy lips, a wide forehead and a beautiful jawline tapering into a narrow chin. But somehow I always felt her face canvass was very ephemeral. One moment she would be exhuming warmth and a stillness of being soothing the looker to the core and the very next moment she could look utterly vulnerable.

And that came from her eyes. There was something about them. Some understated but deeply hallucinating melancholy. She could speak through her eyes and later as we got to know each other better, I sometimes felt she had much to say, many untold stories, which she never shared with anyone.

However, unperturbed by the rejection I took the initiative, and so did Walter and soon we started to talk, initially both of us separately with Julie but eventually after a few days all three of us together.

The more we talked, the more we had to share and in due course of time we became best buddies, doing normal things which friends do- hanging out, going for movies and parties and enjoying other such innocent pleasures of life together. It stayed that way even when later on just before graduating from school Julie proposed to Walter and they became a couple and I-a common friend.

I threw a big party for them which many of our close mates attended and almost all of them teased me that my best buddy was running away with my girl, but I was really happy for them, as they were two people from my life with whom I was really close and I knew they were madly in love with each other.

Just watching them together was an exercise in sheer joy. It made me happy.

After school our lives took us in different directions. I went to pursue my Engineering at *Columbia* and Walter his graduation in Physics from *Virginia* and Julie went to *Yale* to graduate in Music as she always wanted to be a musician.

Yes, if you walk down Wall Street and go to the school of music on College Street and look at the scroll of honor there, you will find the name *Julie Edmonds* right at the top of the class of 1987.

Our vacation planning ensured being together at least twice every year even if it could be only for a couple of days. Of course for Walter and Julie, two love birds on fire, this was as much about wild passions as it was about our friendship bonds, but for me who had still not found that special person, it was only and only about having a fantastic time with my buddies.

I was not into any serious relationship and always had a new girlfriend by my side when we went camping to various jungles and beaches. You can say your dad was in search of true love at the time so he was exploring.

That was till the time I met Nancy at *Columbia* at her freshman party during my sophomore year where a friend of mine had dragged me. I guess you are well aware of our love story, but what I want to tell you is that when Nancy joined me on my next vacation with my buddies, the four of us were like a mad house on fire and it was on one such trip to *Jacksonville* during my pre-final year that I proposed to her and unlike my last experience at school, this time I wasn't rejected.

All four of us really fit in and those were the most memorable years of my life when we literally blew *Florida* beaches- partying, surfing, fishing, having wild nights and going camping in two cosy tents.

Four friends, *two* couples, all madly in love with each other and of course very-very high on life.

I and Walter differed from each other on many things as we were two different personalities. Walter was an extremely focused guy who wanted to excel in everything he did and I was more of a chilled out person who preferred taking it easy in life. But there was one thing which united us like none other, and that was our shared passion to become a fighter pilot. This passion got further ignited when in 1986 *Top Gun* got released and Tom Cruise did those impossible looking acrobatics in his F14. Just like *Maverick* and *Goose* in the movie, here were two buddies with those soaring dreams in their eyes, to touch the horizon in a fighter plane.

Both of us applied for the OCC (Officer's Candidate Course) and as luck would have it we both got selected. At the end of the *ten* week course, we got commissioned as *Second Lieutenants* on the very same day and one of the proudest moments for both of us was when after the formal commissioning ceremony, we- the newly commissioned Lieutenants, had our own pinning ceremony where Nancy pinned to my uniform the gold insignia bar of a second lieutenant and Julie did the honors for Walter.

Some dreams when they come true make us believe that we are one step closer to the higher good in our life and this was one such dream. We drenched ourselves completely in the elixir that night like there was no tomorrow. It was a night to rejoice, to welcome the future, to become one with the one loved. And we did exactly that.

The coincidences which followed after this some-times made me wonder perhaps Walter and I had a *"karmic connection"* with each other, as after finishing the basic school both of us indicated the *Air MOS* as our Military Occupational Specialty, and again- we both got selected for it.

Eventually two best friends were picked for advanced training on the multirole fighter F/A-18C to get des-ignated as Marine Corps Pilots. It was an absolute honor to be inducted into the *Blue Angel* flight demonstration squadron and it was the week after in-duction when I got hitched to your mom and flew to Bahamas for our honeymoon.

Within a span of *three* weeks I accomplished *three* ma-jor goals of my life- getting into the *Blue Angels*, get-ting married to the love of my life and having my honeymoon at Bahamas. Sometimes life is on a giving spree. It was one such time of my life.

In August of 1991 we were assigned to a *Carrier Air Wing* under different Strike Fighter Squadrons at Nav-al Air base *Oceana* when *Iraq* invaded and annexed *Kuwait*. US was at the vanguard of discussions with Iraq and all of us had an inkling some real action might be round the corner. Our combat preparations started and on 28th December 1991 our battle group was deployed in *Operation Desert Storm* to kick *Saddam* forces out of *Kuwait* and to stop him from progressing into *Saudi Arabia*. Our sorties were launched from the *Persian Gulf* and from the Saudi base.

A soldier by nature and by conditioning is valorous, trained to execute orders without asking any questions about the veracity of the task. But sometimes reality is so big and daunting that it gets in the soldiers way. And when that happens valor hangs from the fingertips of reality. What was initially thrilling became nerve wrecking after some time and it was not the fear of getting killed in the war which makes me say this. It was something else building up slowly, seeping into our thoughts which in due course of time gripped us with a haunting intensity.

Collateral Damage!

Bringing the enemy down in a combat zone is what a soldier trains himself for, and getting the enemy swiftly with precision gets him glory. But precision in warfare is more of an implication than exactitude despite the sophistry of modern warfare with all the reconnaissance and satellite imagery based guidance of missiles and weapons. There can be multitude of reasons behind this like error of judgment in the exact enemy coordinates or some technical error or sometimes panic based carpet bombing of enemy territory or the enemy itself placing its forces camouflaged around civilian areas making it impossible for the invading party to isolate the civilians from the professional fighters.

Whatever be the reason, the end result is always the same.

Collateral Damage!

So as a combatant, say as a pilot, you go out for a sortie, fire at the enemy- a bomb or a missile, and sometimes in the process along with the enemy you also bring down a bunch of civilians. You don't realize it then, but when you see it afterwards with *twenty-four* hours of CNN blaring in your face, each square inch of the battlefield, you try to shrug it off telling yourself "What Can I do? I did my duty. This happens sometimes".

And despite the political garble or any other mumbo-jumbo offering rationalizations, the fact remains that even for the most valiant and cold blooded warrior it's difficult to withstand what collateral damage does to the soldier's psyche....eventually. Because in every soldier's life comes a time when he is alone, face to face with himself.

And that's when it gets to him. Now of course some survive the guilt, the horror but most of them (including the decorated ones and the best of the soldiers) sometimes suffer really hard.

Most of us at the theater avoided talking about the subject as it made life all the more difficult but both me and Walter often shared with each other whatever we went through. He suffered more because of his courage to be more naked with himself in seeing the truth as compared to his compatriots there. Walter was as courageous in facing the bane of life as he was passionate in pursuing his dreams.

But passion is a strange thing. It is high-affinity stuff for everything which follows its origin. There are circumstances when it qualifies to be the original sin.

I don't know many people who find true love in school and then have a *"crazy-perennially-increasing-in-intensity-with-each-passing-year"* kind of love life. That comes only from a very passionate soul.

I was a damn good pilot myself, proud of my sorties and spins and loops and personally know many great pilots. But Walter was a class apart. By nature and by training a pilot has to be supremely confident, highly skilled in his craft, and you won't find one lacking in these traits but Walter was a maverick. He could leverage his plane to deliver a bit more, raising the bar every-time for all of us. And he did all this from a never ending storehouse of passion.

But as I said, passion is a strange thing. It gives you the focus to be relentless in your pursuits but then, nothing in this world comes alone. It's always a package, so being relentless in life also gets you things which you don't want and which sometimes are antithesis of what you had pursued in the first place.

You are passionate about landing in a cushy high paying Wall Street job, fine you can have it, but it would seldom come alone. The high paying stuff would come bundled with an 80 hr. (+) week which could possibly mean *no time for family*.

You fancy being the best pilot in the whole squadron as that gives you a feeling of fulfillment. Fine you can be that pilot if you are skilled and gifted enough and train really hard but it won't end just there. For there could be times when your flirting with danger, going into enemy territory, hitting targets with precision could take some lives which were not meant to be taken.

Simply put, you can't pick and choose only that what you want from life, as life is not as simple as choosing a flavor of ice-cream.

Walter razed many a SAM (surface to Air Missiles) and enemy aircraft to ground, but he also inflicted maximum collateral damage in the process.

He was particularly bothered about killing an Iraqi family in one of his successful operations which got widely covered on television, *"Carnage from sky- War consumes entire family"*. These and other similar captions showing mangled remains of what once used to be a *happy* family highlighting the atrocities of war. He somehow felt there was too much of blood on his hands- innocent blood, and being his closest friend I knew he was never the same person after that.

Two days after this Iraqi family episode Walter received a letter from Julie bringing him the news that she was pregnant. It's hard to put into words what I saw in his eyes that day. His happiness was like mist which envelopes everything it touches in its embrace.

He wrote a letter to Julie and we had a long chat after that. He was very happy but I could sense there was something which bothered him a lot. When I asked him what the matter was, this is what my friend told me.

"I am very happy James, but I am also scared. I know this is the biggest moment of my life but sometimes I have a premonition something bad is going to happen. When I close my eyes I see them- that family, those parents and two small kids. They look at me and smile as if I they are trying to say how I can have all that happiness for myself which I took away from them".

"Come on Walts! You had an earmarked target and don't forget you were just doing your duty. These things happen sometimes in a war and nothing can be done about it", but I knew I could not take that feeling out of him. It stayed.

That was the last conversation I had with my friend in the theater as two days after this, his F/A-18C was taken down by an Iraqi Surface to Air Missile. He ejected at the last moment and for the next fourteen days nothing was known about him. His status became MIA (Missing in action) and it was only after two weeks the coalition reconnaissance group came to know that he was taken a Prisoner of War by the Iraqi troops.

Walter was a prize- catch for the Iraqis and they tried their best to elicit strategic information out of him. When the standard torture methods could not deduce anything they improvised. When finally he was rescued by the American reconnaissance forces even the battle-hardened rescue team soldiers were shocked to see the state he was in. In those final moments he took many bullets, some from his captors before they were razed to the ground and probably some from the barrage of mortar, bombs and bullets which came from the attacking coalition forces.

It was ironic that this time he was the *collateral damage*.

They transported him to the *Command Hospital for Gulf War Soldiers* in an extremely critical condition with bullets and splinters in his body and fracture in his legs and majority of his skin lacerated. He also had multiple abdominal injuries and tissue damage as one of the bullets damaged his liver, stomach and the left kidney.

He went through multiple rounds of abdominal surgery and despite doing their best; doctors had little hope for him. But call it his zeal to live and survive against all odds or call it Julie's love for him which gave him strength, he endured the initial rounds of surgery done in the war zone and after a couple of weeks was shifted to USA and Julie who was more than four months pregnant fainted when she saw Walter.

Naval hospital Virginia received him in an extremely serious condition and unlike many other soldiers he was lucky enough to survive with such grievous injuries. His abdominal injuries posed a great risk for infection to recur. But as love has great healing power so on the fifth day of his arrival he spoke a few words for the first time. He was still heavily sedated with lots of tubes coming out of his body but that day, regaining consciousness he suddenly woke up, and asked for Julie.

For next five days Julie was his shadow. She would sit by his side talking to him for hours, making plans about the baby's arrival and their future together. Sometimes I and Nancy would also join them as Walter was now shifted to a private room and the four of us would reminisce about the days of thunder which we had in the past and which we now so much looked forward to have, as soon as life would allow it.

Nancy and Julie were good friends but they became really close during this period as Julie would tell Nancy so many things about Walter, the way he cared for her when they stayed together in happier times, how he would always go that extra mile to ensure those sweet little things which make life happy.

Julie would tell us what plans Walter had for the child and the name he had selected- *Sarah*, in case it was a girl. Being with Julie and Walter gave me and your mom some of the most beautiful moments of our life. The way they cared for each other, Julie through her nurturing of Walter who could not move or speak much, but would look at her with so much of love in his eyes which would make words superfluous. He was visibly drunk on her love. There was always something going on between them, something so beautiful and pure that it was impossible not to be affected by it. And affected we got- me and Nancy, as love has a rub-on effect, and it was during this period my relationship with Nancy got totally transformed and we forged those bonds which are there for a lifetime.

But one day suddenly Walter developed very high fever and woke up complaining of severe pain in his abdomen. They immediately shifted him back to the ICU and his scans showed internal bleeding in the stomach with the hemoglobin level dropping drastically. Few more tests and countless CTs and scans diagnosed that although the bullets were removed from his stomach, but because of the ricocheting bullet he had internal organ damage and his spleen was getting severely affected which caused the trouble now.

The very next day he was again shifted back to the OT going under the knife one more time. This time he came out extremely weak and was in pain for many days thereafter. He remained in the ICU under observation for several days and unlike last time his recovery this time was very slow. For next one month he would be shifted to his private room for a few days but some complication would come up and again they would put him in the ICU.

For all of us the disquietude stemming from our abject helplessness in bringing any comfort to Walter was rapidly escalating into a never ending trauma and there were times when Julie would simply break down not having a clue as to what to do. On 1st May 1991 they shifted him back to his room and for next couple of days he looked quite normal and even talked for many hours sitting on his bed and that day when he went to the washroom on his own all of us thought now the soldier would fight it out as he was back on his feet, finally.

But again after two days he developed fever and this time his tests brought grave news. He had intra- abdominal abscess and was going into sepsis. They again moved him to the OT and went for a colon removal surgery, not once but two times in as many weeks. His condition was becoming quite precarious and all throughout this period he was very weak to talk.

All this had a heavy toll on Julie. She was under tremendous stress and her blood pressure shot up. Doctors advised her to take complete rest but she would not listen to anybody and was virtually on her toes most of the times.

Walter was now under observation and after about ten days from his last operation he again got up from his bed and with Julie's support walked a few steps. For next couple of days he would daily walk for a few minutes inside his room under the physiotherapist's guidance. One day while walking inside the room he stumbled and was about to fall but the *physio* caught hold of him. He complained of a tingling sensation and numbness in his legs. At first everybody thought it might be because of tissue and muscle weakness because of being bedridden for quite some time but then it became progressive and he was again shifted for a CT. They diagnosed there were some very minute splinters around his spine which quite strangely were not diagnosed before and which had damaged certain nerves in his spinal area. The condition was quite dangerous and critical as per the head of surgery at Virginia Hospital.

They did many tests on him and on 15th July 1991 after an examination by a panel of doctors Walter was told one final operation was required to take out the minute splinters lodged in his spinal area but it was a call which he had to take. Without the operation there were little chances he would ever be able to stand on his feet again, but even if he went under the knife the risk of a complete paralysis was fifty percent.

Sometimes for a fighter pilot 50% is a good enough chance to go for. I still vividly remember the conversation which Walter had with Julie, with all of us around having small talks. Moments when your heart knows about the danger lurking ahead, but yet you put your faith in whatever you believe in.

"Everything is going to figure out Julie, don't you worry." He said looking at Julie with a smile on his face.

"It has to. I'll give you maximum a month to get up from this bed. You have a lot of work to do Lieutenant. I hope you remember all those promises you made, about pampering me no end." Julie replied, trying to put up a brave face in front of Walter.

And that brought a wide smile on my friend's face and he said, "When those Iraqi assassins could not get me, this is just a small piece of metal above my ass. I'll come shining through."

"Of course you will. And then you will give me a massage every day and then we'll take bath together and then you'll feed me and won't say a word when I throw tantrums, OK. Just get up soon Walts, am waiting for it." Julie said taking Walter's face between her palms.

And then Walter said something out of the blues. "Let's get married Julie. Let's get married NOW! "

Julie, like all of us, was taken by surprise and she wanted to say something, but then she chose to let it go and smiled and looked at me with a questioning look on her face.

"Yes, I think it can be arranged", is all I said and walked out of the room to arrange for a wedding in that hospital room.

The next morning, my buddies got married right in the middle of that room in which I was the best-man and Nancy the bridesmaid and Grace, Julie's mother, gave the customary walk to Julie giving her hands in Walter's hands.

Walter was operated on 24th July 1991 and the doctors were not very sure if it was a success. In the words of the Chief Surgeon *Dr. Kane Harris* "There is something about his case which is beyond explanation. Things look well and in control but his body is not responding the way it should and there is absolutely no reason why it shouldn't. I am not sure out here, but there is something which we are not able to figure out, looks like he was subjected to some expos-

ure out there in the war doing something to his system, but it might be pure conjecture too, as I don't
have any reasonable basis to claim that, at least not
yet".

They put him in critical care and after about a week
when they did some more tests on him all hell broke
loose. Despite their best efforts, the doctors could
not prevent him from going into complete paralysis
of his lower limbs. He had no sensation left in his legs
and was completely crippled waist down.

I was shocked to see him in that state but for Julie it
was like her whole world had collapsed. She did not
utter a single word and just stared blankly ahead. I
could see behind her exterior personae of optimism
lay an abyss of darkness and I was afraid she was
reaching the inflection point. Walter was still uncon-
scious when Julie went hysterical going in a deep
shock. Our whole world was getting razed to ground,
inch by inch, and none of us had any clue how to save
it.

I cursed myself for the knowing. I cursed myself for
seeing the flame of life getting extinguished day by
day and I cursed myself for being so abjectly helpless
about it not able to do anything which could have
reversed the wheels of destiny.

But I also saw something else...

I saw two souls completely entwined with each other
despite all odds, despite the sultry and spasmodic pain

of looming separation, despite the anguish of destiny gnawing at the hopes of a lovely future.

And in the middle of this anguish I saw the power of two souls to bear the pain with dignity, in each other's arms, strengthening each other moment by moment, silently savouring the unutterable memories of moments spent together.

On 10th of August 1991 Julie went into premature labor three weeks before her due date. She was rushed to the OT where a Cesarean section delivered her baby into this world and the moment the umbilical was cut she had a massive cardiac arrest.

Despite a team of doctors trying their best to revive her, she could not be saved and on 11th August night at 11:55 PM, Julie, my best friend's wife, passed away. She was no more and all I could feel was *black* infinite darkness in the world and inside my soul.

The lights went out forever...

I felt as though I was falling into a bottomless pit, an abyss with no end. The sheer enormity of the loss just made me numb and I was absolutely clueless about how to carry on. How could this happen? How could God or whosoever moved this world be so cruel to strike such a loving family with two horrible blows one after the other? It was beyond my capacity to handle what struck us and the doctors thought about putting me on sedatives.

But I gathered my wits as there were immediate things to attend to, and just the thought of breaking the news to Walter raised my heckles. I felt even if I could plug into all the courage which existed in this world, it would not suffice to give me the guts to break the news to Walter who had regained consciousness after his surgery. But there was no option. I had to tell him and that too immediately as he had asked for me and Nancy many times after regaining consciousness.

When I felt it was no longer possible to ignore facing Walter, I gathered myself and went to his room. He lay on his back with his eyes closed, lost in his world. After a while he opened his eyes and looked at me and smiled.

"Julie, How is she....How is my child...Boy or Girl? Where were you...called you so many times...?"

My heart came to my mouth and all could say was, "Boy"

And then I could not control myself and keeping my head on his pillow. I cried.

Walter thought I was getting emotional because of his condition, his paralysis and he put his hand on my head in order to console me and said "Don't worry, I'll be OK. The doctor told me they are working on something, which is not yet approved by FDA and is at trial stage. I'll go for it, who knows..."

And then he asked again. "How is Julie?"

I raised my head from his pillow and in that moment, in that very moment he must have seen it in my eyes and that brought a look on his face which stopped my heart.

It was such a frozen look.

I had never seen such a look on a man's face before, frozen in time, frozen in space. It was like looking at darkness itself, like lights going out in this world and darkness descending on earth. It was like looking at the remains of a prehistoric structure with all life gone, long back.

That look which I saw on my friends face that day got etched in my memory forever.

And then my buddy, my alter ego and my best companion in my life journey howled. One which comes from the soul, from the glimpse of all he must have lived in the past and the death of all he must have aspired to live in the future- which he saw no more. In that moment I witnessed a whole world dying and that cry from Walter just tore through my soul as I could feel it was the end of his "*being*", and whatever else he had.

He was in a state of profound shock and the doctor immediately sedated him putting him to sleep.

Next few days he was absolutely silent and wished to be left alone and for the first time in my life my entire belief system was shaken. I was never a very religious person but sometimes we bring the existence of God into context just to vent out our anger against something which is beyond our powers to rectify or control. My heart wept for my friend who lost everything he ever valued for in his life- his love Julie, his dream to fly and serve his country and the most tragic part was he could not even grieve properly as how do you do that when you are paralyzed.

He could not go and touch Julie. As his son was born premature he could not take him in his hands and kiss him and tell him he loved him and together they would try to make a good life remembering Julie and cherishing her memories. He could not do anything which could bring him comfort, simple acts like going for a walk or going to that room which was full of his memories with Julie.

He was forced to just lie on his back and think and wait for moments to pass. What else could be more tragic than enduring that in such a condition?

Nancy and I ensured one of us was always around him but Walter completely withdrew into a world where nothing existed for him. He shut himself completely off from all of us.

Then after a few days he called for me and told me he wanted to see his son as the nurse told him now the child was much better and could be brought to his room for a short duration. I was so happy and excited; I ran for the nursery and in ten minutes straight was back with the baby in the nurse's arms. Walter looked at his child and smiled with his lips quivering to say something and his eyes misty with pearls of happiness. I could feel the floodgates inside him raring to go and the moment I placed the baby in his lap, my friend could not contain himself any more.

This was to be the most precious moment of his life which he and Julie must have dreamt of celebrating together, but the way it turned out in those moments, took my faith away from me, forever.

At least that's what I thought in those moments.

He kissed his son gently and smiled through the stream of tears flowing down his eyes. His son smiled back at him and suddenly got very excited at something, throwing his legs around the way babies do, and then he just raised his hand and with his tiny fingers caught hold of Walter's fingers and started to laugh, real hard. He laughed and Walter laughed back and seeing that his son just went rapturous. He was thoroughly enjoying himself and for a moment all of us in that room forgot what life had thrown at us during past couple of days.

We left them alone so that they could spend some time with each other. After a while Walter called for me and asked for the baby to be shifted to the nursery. The nurse and Nancy took the baby away and when both of us were alone Walter spoke to me.

"James, you need to do me a favor".

"Anything brother, anything, just tell me". I said.

"Please tell me frankly James, what are my chances? Will I ever be able to stand on my feet again? I feel like I have tons of lead inside my body and my mouth and in every pore of my body and it hurts like hell. I feel nothing in my legs, absolutely nothing, but I want to live James. I want to fight and stand up again. I want to see my son grow up and I want to be around him when he goes to the school. I have to. I don't know how, but I have to. Julie must be watching us from there and I know she wants me to fight and I want to fight too. I want to James, for my kid. Please do something. I want to give it all I have so that my son does not grow up as an orphan the way his father did.

Please help me James."

And then he cried and I just did not have the heart to console him. I just could not, but I held his hand in mine and waited for him to take out that pain through his eyes, as much as he could.

He fought valiantly for next two months, gave it all he had but there was something about his body, his once healthy and a *marine-pilot-fit-body* which was not right. Something had happened to him physically. The will was intact but the body was not what it should have been, even taking into account all the injuries which he took.

Walter's condition deteriorated progressively and he went into multiple organ failure and was put on ventilator support for a couple of days. He would respond to the heavy dosage of antibiotics and would be taken off the machine for next couple of days but again the infection would hit and they would put him back on the ventilator. This went on for a couple of weeks.

One day when Walter was off the ventilator he called me and told me this.

"Please listen to me.... carefully........ James....... I know.... you love me...... and there is no one else...... who would understand this......so please...... listen...I ask you...... for the biggest favor .....For I have no one else James.........it's only you....nobody else........."

I just held his hand in mine and nodded.

This is what he told me in broken words. "You know both my parents died when I was five years old and I grew up more or less like an orphan. Went into foster care couple of times but it didn't work out but finally I was lucky to meet some really wonderful people in my life who saved me to some extent. I don't want my child to suffer the way I did."

And then he said, "I want him to have the complete experience of both a loving father and a loving mother, parents who can give him so much of love and care that he grows up without any bottled up feelings in his heart, actually cherishing his journey. I want him to have the completeness of experience as far as growing up is concerned.

I want you to adopt my son James, you and Nancy. I don't have anybody in this world. Will you do that James? Will you take him as your son? Tell me, will you love him and give him all that I and Julie wanted to give him."

My heart was crushed, because of him, his agony, his pain, and I completely understood what he said.

"Of course Walter, I will. I and Nancy will be so glad to have him as our son, but I am pretty sure we'll get you back on your feet."

I knew that he knew that both of us knew the truth. Time was slipping out of our hands and there was not much of a hope and he smiled looking at me.

A smile which says, "thank you friend for being there, but both of us know that the time has come."

"I want the adoption formality to be done away with as soon as possible...Please James...get it done..."

Walter had a resolve of steel and because of his insistence the complete legal formalities were done in straight one month.

And that was how Peter, my son, that your father Walter, the most amazing person in this world, gave you, his heart, his soul to us, so that you could have all that he wanted you to have .

I know it is hard for you to come to terms with this fact now, through this letter, but believe me son, there was no other way. That amazing son of a gun, your dad Walter had planned even the timing of this.

Next couple of days Walter spent all his waking moments with you, talking to you, telling you so many stories about Julie, your Mom. He did all this to save you, to give you a life which you could be proud of.

He passed away when you were three months old. He loved you more than anything else in this world, as much as he loved Julie. It's important for you to know son that your father fought like a true soldier till the very end. He never gave up and despite knowing that he was losing it every single day, he kept on fighting and he did it only for you, notwithstanding that he lost the biggest battle of his life in the end.

He truly believed you had me and Nancy to take care of you and the biggest medal which I have in my life is the trust which your father, my dear friend put in me and your Mom. In the end he knew his time had come but he was not sad. He was not sad because he felt he would be uniting with Julie.

That night of 14th Nov he passed away peacefully in his sleep. He just went away.

Couple of days before passing away, he had a conversation with me in which he asked me to do two things.

First one was not to tell you anything about him and Julie till your graduation day. He said your soul in its growing up years should not feel the pain and agony of loss of parents.

And second thing he told me was to give you a letter from him. But that was to be given only on your graduation day and not before that.

As I said the only religion I know of, *Love*, was taught to me by Walter and Julie. And as your father I know you too were canonized in that.

Love you Peter. Wish I could change what ever happened.

Sometimes I think their story could have ended in hundreds of other ways instead of the way it did, but then I also know in all things esoteric in life, the one which is most mystical is love.

There is no logic to what happens in love because logic can't get you there in first place, only a strange kind of madness can. A madness to surrender yet conquer, a searing intensity to "be" and "become" one and mingle like drops do in an ocean. And what comes out of this madness is an unceasing and insatiable urge to commune with the one you love.

Now that makes every story different- the way people define and live their madness.

Each and every moment of Julie and Walter's life was smeared with this urge to be and become one with each other and that's why they lived the way they did. And perhaps that's why their story ended the way it did, so that they could be with each other someplace else.

It's hard to understand it from the outside but you'll be able to understand it a bit, if and when you have your own share of madness in life.

I know you will one day. I know it for sure. After all you are his son!

Your Dad.

James

4th

From Walter to Peter

You've kept track,

of my every toss and turn

through the sleepless nights,

each tear entered in your ledger,

each ache written in your book.

Psalm 56:8.

Letter from Walter to Peter

10th October 1991, Jacksonville, FL

Dear Peter,

Do one thing son. Before reading any further just hold this letter really close to your heart, so close that I can feel you and listen to your heartbeat, notwithstanding this unbridgeable chasm of a few decades between us.

Being off the heart-lung machine since past three days makes me feel like a million bucks and today I took full advantage of it by emotionally blackmailing Helena, my caretaker, forcing her to transfer you out of your pram onto my bed for a few minutes. I want you to read this letter with the same look in your eyes which you had a couple of minutes ago lying by my side on my motorized bed which Helena had set to an upright-back position, making it possible for me to hold you and cuddle you.

And that's what I did. I cuddled you and listened to your heartbeat as you lay by my side giggling and kicking the air non-stop with your cute little legs. I wanted to talk to you about so many things but when I tried doing the same, somehow I couldn't. I thought maybe I don't have the energy in me today to speak, but suddenly a thought came to my mind which scared me like someone trapped at the bottom of a well running out of light and air.

"What if I never get a chance to speak again, to share with you all that I want to?" My inner voice told me that chances of this happening were quite bright.

But you are barely a year old and there is no way you are going to understand all that I have to say till you grow up.

And then I asked you "S h a l l... I.... w r i t e..... t o.... y o u.... s o n?

You giggled...

"W i l l... ...y o u ..f e e l.... m e... t h r o u g h... m y.... w o r d s?

You giggled again...

And I knew what to do. I feel that even if you read this after many-many years, I'll know it. You just have to hold it close to your heart.

Before I move ahead let me tell you that Helena, James & Nancy look after me really well and if it weren't for them I don't know what would have I done? It's only because of people like them that the words like faith exist as it is faith and faith alone, which made this possible.

Faith, what I had in James, when I wrote this and asked him to give it to you when you pass out of a college and as these words get delivered to you today, when you read this letter, that faith gets vindicated proving once again that my belief in my friend was well placed. And for me, this is simply incredible as only in the redeeming of this faith could I reach you and share a part of me with you. My only chance to do that, and I love James for making it happen.

Please thank him for this and give him a big hug from my side and also tell him he is the best friend they ever made anywhere on this planet. He is a rock-star and I love him for everything. Tell him if there is anything like redemption, then mine and Julie's would be only because of two people- your dad James and your beautiful mom Nancy, who polished this raw gem .

Now let me admit at the outset that as I write, I am both overwhelmed as well as nervous and the reason is simple. Despite my singular longing to live my life with you, I feel that at the most I would be able to out-dare maybe next couple of nights. I can already smell those first rays of dawn sailing upon the morning wind and the bird of my life preparing to leave this nest to soar on a flight against the sun. The final flight!

Which means for me this is not just a letter but my one and only connection with you in lieu of the love which I wanted to give to you, the life which I wanted to share with you, to see you grow into a handsome hunk which I am sure you must be as you read this.

This letter is all that and much more to me and I don't know if I would be able to tell you all that I want to, considering I don't have much time left to collect my thoughts.

But somewhere deep inside I also feel assured, because I know from my experience there is one thing we can never get enough of, and in the end that is the only thing which actually counts, which gives life all or any of its profundity. Something which I learned from that amazing person-your mom, who gave me all those moments which one needs to understand the secret sauce of life.

That ageless and timeless emotion called Love.

And that's why I feel assured because I know love. I know it from all those moments when it was with me; making everything I had- worthwhile. I am sure I'll be able to pass this gift to you and you'll be able to feel what touched your parents' life.

But first of all, Congratulations, because your reading this letter means your graduation day is round the corner and you are about to enter a sparkling new chapter of your life. So kudos for making the choices you made and let me tell you a secret- they are the best choices as you made them for yourself.

God gave you not one but two set of loving parents and that my son is a blessing. Nancy and James I know must have done a wonderful job in raising you, and whatever you are today is because they believed in you giving you the love which made you the person you are today. I am sure they showed you how to live from the heart because I know this buddy of mine when he makes a promise, he keeps it.

But now I guess is the right time for you to know about your other set of parents too, who brought you into this world and who wanted to live with you with as much love- nurturing you, caring for you, feeding you, walking on the beach with you, with your baby feet leaving those marks on the sand which your mom would have captured in a camera to show to her mom and her friends afterwards..

I met your mom in school and something told me she is the one. I don't know what it was, but she just melted me and it did wonders to my ego to know that the feeling was mutual. She was the best thing which ever happened to me in my life. Knowing your mom and living those many years with her gave me one of the biggest things life can offer- *freedom to be myself*. I was lucky to have a life partner like your mom.

It's hard for me to put into words what I feel for her, because the way a man sees his woman, the way he knows her, the way he feels for her cannot be explained in words.

She was a friend-a pretty caring one, but could give me nightmares if I ever stepped onto her territory. She was my partner in countless jaunts, adventures, misadventures but could pull my ears if she differed with me on the way-to-go about it. She laughed with me like no one else did and could make me laugh pulling me out of ditch of any depth but she could also make me cry so very easily. She would do absolutely anything to make me happy but could also hurt me at times. We were two ordinary people like millions of others leading pretty normal life, doing normal things experiencing pain and pleasure, ups and downs, bane and boon of life together, but one thing which I feel was extraordinary about us was our love for each other and I must say her contribution far outweighed mine in getting us the life we lived together.

She gave me unfathomable love, making it the mainstream of our combined existence and making everything else peripheral. She taught me how to live from the depths shunning the brim.

In my short life I experienced extremes- of love, of valor and violence in the craziest parts of the world and I can tell you that when my eyes will close in those moments of ultimate truth, I would be at peace and the only reason for that would be the love which I got in my life. Even a few moments of true love can make a life worthwhile and if I am ever given the chance to live my life again, I would without doubt make the same choices again even if it'll mean dying young once more.

Be mad, at least once, to fall in love, to experience the insanity of losing yourself to the other. I say so because love is like that, at least when you experience it for the first time. It consumes you, dissolving everything that's yours into the world of your lover. You just want to devour till you find those moments which can potentially give you all that you were looking for in life and if you are lucky enough to reach that zone you will find that beyond this madness, beyond these unflinching winds of passions, of moorings of making it out- exploring, seducing and taking all that she has to give, after the raging flames of passion collide and quench their thirst and get extinguished; beyond all of this you get a choice to get actually fulfilled, a choice to get free forever. But this comes only from the ashes of those flames of passion.

If you reach there, you'll know for yourself- your heart will tell you if you listen to it. And perhaps that's the pursuit of real happiness- To Love with your heart and your soul.

Reaching there is enough for a life- any life; and everything else is either incidental or inconsequential.

I understand this must have brought too much of pain into your heart, knowing about me and Julie, the way everything turned out. But let me tell you son, don't let that pain seep into your heart and you must not for a moment feel sorry about us, about me and your mom. You know why I say that? I say so because both I and your mom had the most fantastic times together right from our middle school days till she left for where everybody goes one day.

Death after all is not that big a deal it is made out to be, but living the life of your dreams certainly is. That's where most of the people fail and that's where I and your mom passed with flying colors.

Consider this.

As I write this to you, there are about 5.4 billion people on this planet and I read about a very interesting study done by a population scientist who calculated roughly 105 billion people have lived on our planet in total since the time *Homo sapiens* came into existence. And obviously every single one of them had to pack up and leave when their time was up, so death is not something which happened only to Julie or would happen in due course to me. It happens to thousands of people daily so there's no big deal about it.

The point is with death as the common denominator and with belief, religion, profession, wealth, time, place, era, and countless other differentiators in these billions of lives, only those who had the courage to live their dreams for whatever time they were here, had solace in their heart at the time of crossing over, at the time of finishing the journey and going into the unknown.

You can take pride in the fact that your parents lived that kind of life, so rejoice son, for there is no reason for you to feel sad.

And I must say I thoroughly enjoyed my innings here as life was extremely generous for most part of it, to me and to my love Julie in giving all that we asked for. So be sure of asking what you actually want out of your life because most certainly you'll get what you'll ask for. That is if you ask it with complete honesty.

Ask your dad James and he'll tell you how crazy we were- I and Julie, never letting anything stop us from going after wackiest of the ideas either one of us had.

She was a total sport in anything and everything and over the years both of us learned the art of being blissfully insane in pursuing our desires- adventure sports of every conceivable kind, long jungle trails, painting the town red partying, reading our favorite books together, going on long hitch-hiking tours, doing creative art workshops, and many other pursuits of the heart.

We gave life our best shot and were a robust pillar of support for each other's craziness. I was ambitious and so was she and we were pretty serious when it came to pursuing our professional goals and all those things which give you a career, but we could somehow always distill the esoteric from the mundane. We learned to pursue happiness together and could somehow always steal those moments from life for us. Julie firmly believed life happens in the middle of all such moments which add up to hours, weeks or years, but we live in moments, in the NOW and not in aggregations of them and that's why she said it was important to enjoy every single one of them and that's why till the time we were here, we enjoyed it thoroughly.

And we could do this only because of each other, because we had love in our life and when you have love in your life, including that amorous-raw-pulsating-passion (because after all even that is a source of bliss if it comes out of love), it gives you a perspective to enjoy all that comes afterwards, and if you are lucky enough then sometimes you go beyond all that is transient and momentary to reach deep within yourself and your partner, exploring the true hidden gems life has to offer.

The biggest lesson which I learned was that life can be a never ending orgy for the mind, body as well as the soul, if its fulcrum is true love and I thank God for sending that angel Julie, as crazy as me, quite early in my life. It made all of my subsequent choices and experiences enjoyable.

So if you have to find something, find love - That special person in your life who brings out the craziness in you. You'll know it when you find her and when you do; it's time to live all that craziness with her. Now that's what we call living in love.

And how do you "be" in true love throughout your life. Once you feel she is the one you love, just be yourself with her. There is no place for any pretensions in love and there is no place for any ego too, so just be what you are and give her complete freedom so that she be what she is, naturally.

It requires some work, but once you start doing it honestly, it comes easily.

And then- communicate.

Communicate throughout your life, and how much or how less is different for everybody but the key is to communicate that much which allows you to "be yourself" giving her the freedom to "be herself" and whenever you feel there are spaces creeping between what you are "being" and what you "really are", rest assured it's time to communicate with your partner.

Believe me, it's as simple as that and it worked perfectly fine for me. The essence is unless you are yourself in a relationship, it will never work out so do whatever it takes for both of you and the elixir would be yours forever!

I also want to tell you something about dreams- the most amazing gift which we have as anything worthwhile always starts with a dream. But nobody tells us how to dream? How to dream the way we eat, sleep or work, so that it becomes organic to our life.

I'll tell you. To go there in the dream world one needs to first disassociate oneself from the flow. One has to shun arrogance of whatever one thinks one has in plenty and has to just witness life with the humility of an observer and think "Is my state of being, my state of doing and my state of progressing in life taking me where I actually want to go? Is this what I want out of my life?"

And this has to be done while being completely disassociated with the aphrodisiacs of peer actions, peer praises, accolades thrown our way, conditioned beliefs and everything else which defines us at that point in time.

Only then true listening starts. What heart wants and what we are destined for.

You might fail to listen to it initially, but if you do it relentlessly, one day you'll start getting it and life would never be the same after that.

Dream this way and you will not end up one day in a relationship, in a career or a profession, in a country, in a setting, and most importantly, in a state of being, which was not meant for you. The whole purpose of life is to eventually be that person, have that life which you want for yourself, one that takes birth and culminates from your own dreams and not from of others- of the society or even of your parents.

So dream and once you get it- go after them with all you have and believe me you'll always get what you look for honestly.

The last thing I want to talk to you is about my theory of *Plusses and Minuses* which I coined one *not-so-fine* evening in the war zone at Iraq, upon returning from a field operation which was adjudged extremely successful.

But was it?

That was the first question which came to my mind when I landed my fighter jet on the tarmac and it was in those moments that I understood about Plusses & Minuses of life.

Every addition (Plus) to your life has the possibility of getting you some minuses, but the problem is it gets revealed only when you look backwards and that's why it's important to do a very simple thing- take a pause and just be present to whatever life decision you might be taking for yourself.

Just be present to it before actually taking it. Having done that if you want to go ahead with it, than just take it with all you've got, firing on all cylinders!

I always dreamt of a career with the armed forces and I worked really hard, doing everything required to realize my dream of becoming a fighter pilot. It took a lot of dreaming followed by a lot of persistent hard work and yes, a bit of luck.

Getting commissioned as a fighter pilot was a major plus to my life.

I trained really hard and in due course of time was a part of the prestigious *Blue Angels* squadron. It felt really great and I was flying high, both literally as well as metaphorically. Then *Gulf War* started and I was one of the most successful fighter pilots in that war and success was measured in terms of hitting the assigned targets with precision, which I did better than the best.

Like everybody else I too believe that it is a great honor to serve one's own country, being at the battlefront giving and taking bullets so that people back home could feel safe and be at peace. So in a way, war is the price which we pay for peace. Being that soldier was a major *plus* to my life, but before joining the forces I had never thought about some others aspects which my choices could get me into.

I killed many people, most of them enemies but not always. Many a times my line of fire terminated upon civilians. It was the biggest Minus to my life, those innocent killings, something which I could never contemplate while planning my career.

That is the problem, of not being able to see the consequences beforehand. My choice to become a fighter pilot was shaped by the *stars and stripes* I would earn, the honor which it'll bring and of course the thrill and adventure of a soldier's life while serving one's nation. But it never occurred to me even once that being a soldier could also mean carrying out a war in some far-fetched land on some god forsaken people who will get in the line of fire which I or others would start. A war at times, whose real intentions could be dubious, possibly thrust upon this world by greed, ego and arrogance of some very powerful people completely alienated from reality. I never once thought I could end up being an instrument for the greed and power play to manifest.

All these Minuses got automatically added to my destiny, to my future the moment I took the decision of becoming a soldier. While making that career decision I never realized that in the end every war is about killing or getting killed. I never understood that the so called honor which winning a war or dying in it brings when a soldier returns either in a body bag, or if lucky then in person, and his fellow countrymen feel proud of him standing by the roadsides, eulogizing epitaphs in his or her honor, is often a very expertly cultured jingoistic emotion fed into the psyche of nationals by demagogues and master at their craft politicians or TRP hungry media- all quite adept at leveraging emotions of an entire country in the name of *"Justice Being Done"*.

Which most of the times is bullshit!! Plain and simple bullshit!

There never was and never will be any honor in a war, EVER.

There is no justice which gets served, EVER.

People Kill each other because some leaders fail to solve some problems which could be solved if a better one was in place or at least if he or she was better advised which greed, ego or arrogance prevent from happening most of the times.

In different times and in a different country, thousands of years ago, after one of the goriest and carnage perpetrating war of the times, a great warrior-ruler on seeing the bloodshed which the war brought understood the abject futility of it.

His name was *Ashoka* which means *painless* or without sorrow, but he was such a bloodthirsty and cruel warrior he was called *Chanda-Ashoka, or Ashoka the Fierce,* but in the battle of Kalinga in which more than a hundred thousand soldiers got killed, Ashoka's walk of victory in the battleground was welcomed by bodies strewn over each other and by the curses and wails of half butchered & limbless waiting-for-death soldiers. Valor and pride of victory in the emperor's heart was replaced by remorse and sorrow at the sight of such a gargantuan slaughter brought upon by the war.

Ashoka was never the same again. He overcame his weakness of winning wars by renouncing all conquests and embracing the path of *Dhamma*, of *Buddha* and walking on that path he was immortalized as the greatest emperor ever born on this planet. He was truly valorous.

But then, those times were different and he was Ashoka.

Today, it's not going to happen son, so it's important when you take any major life decision, when you *Plus* anything major to your life, think it through till the end before acting on it. Don't take it for its perceived value but see that will acting on that choice bring you real happiness (the way you define it) and while doing so also think about everything else which that decision might bring.

What I wrote above is not about choosing Buddhism or religion per se as the panacea to life's obstacles (unless you really want to do that), nor is it about playing safe while taking life decisions. On the contrary it is about living life to the fullest, doing whatever you believe in completely, and chasing it with all guts and gumption no matter whatever it takes. But just keep in mind that a harbinger of peace is much more valorous than a perpetrator of war

It's neither the fear of death nor the agony of saying pack-up pretty young in life which makes me say this, because when a man with love in his heart and soaring dreams in his eyes chooses these stars and stripes, he makes a choice for himself. He chooses a life of valor, of glory like millions of his fellow countrymen knowing fully well that beyond the clarion cry of adventure, beyond the surging desire to serve his country, beyond the metaphors and decorations conferred on his chest by this world, lies a possibility-howsoever distinct, that in the end he might have to give it all, including his life, as a possible repercussion of the choices made by him. He is always aware of it. What I say here is not because I was fortunate or unfortunate enough (the way one looks at it) to be in that arena, getting in the line of fire but what I say here is because of the way it happened to me and the way it happens to thousands of soldiers of US and other armed forces anywhere in the world, year after year after year for unwarranted reasons.

I feel sad the way whims and egos of a powerful minority incapable of solving disputes get imposed on the majority. I feel sad the way armies get used, conflicts get build up, battles get planned, and jingoism gets advocated at the cost of empathy and magnanimity. I feel extremely sad the way lives get brazenly trampled to dust by the wrong decisions of the mighty and powerful, monarchs or elected leaders, sitting in the cool confines of their offices or homes or ranches leaving the "man-in-the-zone" to trample each other and get trampled in return by vagaries of a *could-be-avoided* war.

I feel sad the way a national hysteria gets built-up around an act of horror, an act of myopia, an act of arrogant or failed leadership, and I feel extremely sad the way it happens repeatedly with no lessons learnt ever, with politics getting played turning oppressed nations into mercenaries to get advantage over opposing world-views, to tilt the balance of power and when it gets out of hand then almost always the easy way is chosen propelling young men and women into a supposedly holy war by nations of this world. The whirlpool of politics sucks everything which comes in its way and eventually there are no right or wrong nations, there are only right or wrong people at the helm of affairs who create a battery of annihilation to serve their nefarious ends gobbling generations after generations at this place or that.

So be whatever you want to be, and do whatever gives you happiness, but should you choose to walk on the path of glory like a soldier does, then be truly valorous and spread love, to make this world a bit more beautiful and in harmony with itself because that's the only thing which in future might stop wars and that my son requires a lots of courage.

Which very few people genuinely have.

In the end all goodness in this world comes from people who have it in them to be different, with courage to challenge the status-quo; whatever it takes!

If you become a musician use music to reach out to people's soul to move them, compelling an ego driven war monger leader never to take any half-baked or ill-thought out decision of plunging his country into a war.

If you become an artist, use your art to do that. If you become a corporate and work your way up the ladder, then rest not till you reach a level from where when you speak things happen by way of people listening and politicians leaving their comfort zones. You need not be a crusader unless you want to be one but *have a voice and make it heard.* If people start doing this who knows one day things might change.

Do whatever you do, be whatever you be, but do try a little bit, your bit, whether small or big to prevent somebody from taking a decision of the kind which many a times result in a father writing a letter like this to his son.

And believe me, I might not be the only one writing something like this, meaning you are not the only one reading something like this.

Let's stop things like this from happening again.

Death is inevitable provided it is God-send and not

man-made. It's fair, isn't it?

It's all right if you miss me and Julie sometimes. But never let that pain seep deep into your heart. Let me tell you a secret. Whenever you heart cries out for your parents just stand in front of a mirror and look at yourself and smile. You might see me or Julie in that smile. Or take a deep look into your eyes and you might catch a glimpse of your mom there. Or look at the way you sometimes speak or walk and you might find me walking with you. And when you have a child just watch her or him grow up every day. I promise you, if you do so, you'll stop missing us with pain in your heart.

And son, you don't choose your parents but you can very well choose your friends. The biggest Plus of my life, my biggest treasure were my friends who would do anything for me. What more can I say, hadn't it been for my buddy James and Nancy; you wouldn't be reading this letter today, the way I wanted you to read, near your graduation day.

Can you beat it? Friends can make anything work. I hope you have at least one friend the way I had James. I know it might be too much to ask for, but then as I said earlier, you get what you ask for, so why ask for less?

Have a great life and when you come to visit me and your mom where they must have put us to rest, don't come alone, get your love along.

After all, you have a legacy to preserve...

Your Pa

Walter

Acknowledgments

My sincere thanks to my friends Garima Dhamija, S.P. Singh, Indrani Chakraborty, Anjali Riat, Sandeep Bansal, and Rajesh Das for their insightful comments and timely help with the manuscript review.

Thanks to Sunill Kaushik at Ink Studioz for the cover page design.

Thanks to my beautiful and loving wife, Nandita Chakraborty, for her unconditional love and support and for being there when it mattered the most.

Thanks to my mother for always believing in me, no matter what.

Thanks to the pride and joy of my life, my angel Isha, who is the biggest source of happiness in my life.

And thanks to my dad who lives in me, inspiring me each and every moment. Dad, you were the best…

And thanks to all those whose valour and courage makes the motor of this world run and whose unselfish love give us hope.

A Note on the Author

Vivek Sharma was born in the pink city of India-Jaipur in 1970. After his graduation in Engineering and post-graduation in business administration from Indian Institute of Management Kolkata he worked in various organizations across the globe before settling down at the millennium city- Gurgaon with his childhood sweetheart Nandita- a practicing doctor, his (recently teenaged) daughter Isha, his best buddy-his dad, his mother to whom he owes most of the things in his life and his bundle of joy- Bruno the beagle.

His father's demise two years back was an epoch in his life which took him on a journey to find answers to certain questions. This book came out of him while he was working on something else- his memoir detailing his experiences of his journey. He believes this story found him earlier as it needed to be told earlier.

Four letters of Love is his first book.

Some of his views can be read at his recently started blog worldofvivek.wordpress.com.

He can also be followed on Facebook: www.facebook.com/authorvivek, on

Twitter: @v_vishar and on Gmail: v.vishar@gmail.com

Printed in Dunstable, United Kingdom